To

_____

From

_____

Date

_____

Precious Moments

Christmas play

Text written by
Joanne De Jonge
Illustrated by
Sam Butcher

Welcome
to Our
Program

Baker Books
A Division of Baker Book House Co
Grand Rapids, Michigan 49516

Published by Baker Books
a division of Baker Book House Company
P.O. Box 6287, Grand Rapids, MI 49516-6287

Printed in the United States of America

Library of Congress Cataloging-in-Publication Data

De Jonge, Joanne E., 1943–
    Precious moments Christmas play / illustrated by Sam Butcher : text by Joanne De Jonge.
        p.   cm.
    Summary: Familiar Precious Moments characters present a simple play about the events of the first Christmas.
    ISBN 0-8010-4424-3 (cloth)
    1. Jesus Christ—Nativity Juvenile Fiction. [1. Jesus Christ—Nativity Fiction. 2. Christmas Fiction. 3. Stories in rhyme.]
I. De Jonge, Joanne E. II. Title.
PZ8.3.B9765Pr   1999
[E]—dc21   99-29927

For current information about all releases
from Baker Book House, visit our web site:
http://www.bakerbooks.com

I've got a great idea:
Let's put on a Christmas play!
We'll tell the world that Jesus Christ
was born on Christmas Day.

We'll make some crowns and curtains;
we'll even make our sets.
And when we need some sheep,
why don't we use our pets?

We'll make a little sign
for the road to Bethlehem,
then show how Jesus' parents found
there was no room for them.

And then we'll show the stable,
with "sheep" and "cows" and hay.
We'll tell how when our Lord was born
that's where he had to stay.

Whoever plays the person
who says, "No room to stay,"
can add, "There's room for Jesus
within my heart today."

We'll use a little ladder
to fill the "sky" above
with angels who will sing and tell
the shepherds of God's love.

As angels speak to shepherds
we must be sure to show
they speak to ordinary folks
just like those we know.

When the angels' speech is over
we'll all stand up and say,
"Jesus was born for you and me
on that first Christmas Day."

We'll make a star and move it,
just like God did long ago
to lead the rich, wise travelers
to a land they did not know.

The kids who take the parts
of the wise men in our play
should look and act like people
who came from far away.

And when that scene is over
we'll all stand up and say,
"Jesus was born for others, too,
on that first Christmas Day."

The shepherds and the angels,
the wise men and the star,
all tell us that God sent his Son
for people near and far.

So when the play is over
we'll all stand up and say,
"Jesus was born for everyone
on that first Christmas Day!"

150135   684
                                    To

Torre

Woodworking for kids

Due

| MAY 23 '92 |
| OCT 14 '92 |
| JAN 19 |
| |
| |
| |
| |
| |
| |
| |
| |
| |
| |

WOODWORKING FOR KIDS

WOODWORKING FOR KIDS

FRANK D. TORRE

DOUBLEDAY & COMPANY, INC.

GARDEN CITY, NEW YORK

ISBN 0-385-11430-3 Trade
       0-385-11431-1 Prebound
Library of Congress Catalog Card Number 77–76264
Copyright © 1978 by Frank D. Torre

*Dedicated
to my wife, Betty*

CONTENTS

INTRODUCTION ix

BASIC TOOLS AND HOW TO USE THEM 1
Driving Tools 1
Cutting Tools 5
Shaping Tools 8
Boring Tools 10
The C-Clamp 14
Measuring Tools 15
Fastenings 19

WOOD 23

WOOD FINISHING 25

PROJECTS   **29**

    Baseball Game   **29**

    Bread Slicing Board   **37**

    Chopping Board   **41**

    Perpetual Calendar   **45**

    Bracket and Shelf   **50**

    Adjustable Book Rack   **56**

    Planter with Tiles   **63**

    Ecology Box   **67**

    Coffee Cup Rack   **73**

    Shoeshine Box   **79**

    Desk Organizer   **86**

    Telephone Stand   **94**

    Checkerboard and Checkers   **100**

    Tool Caddy   **107**

    Pipe Rack   **114**

    Birdhouse   **120**

INDEX   **131**

INTRODUCTION

To make something yourself, however "unprofessional," is rewarding. It is a pleasure to master tools and to use them with skill.

There is also another reason why you should learn woodworking. It is fun.

Homemade gifts will give pleasure to both the maker and the recipient, to say nothing of the savings involved.

For this book we have chosen projects you can make easily. Most of them can be made with a few basic tools—saw, hammer, try square, and drill—already available in most homes. We have included a section on the most-used tools and how to use them.

It will be best for you to work with an adult on the projects in this book until you get the knack of handling the tools.

Before you start to build any of the projects, read the complete directions carefully and study the illustrations. If you collect all the necessary materials and tools before you start, it will be much easier for you to follow the step-by-step directions.

Unless you are fortunate enough to have a workbench, the best place to work is probably the kitchen, but ask your parents first. If there is a suitable kitchen table available, measure the top and buy some chipboard of the same size to cover it while you are using it. If not, scout around the secondhand stores for a wood-topped table. Best of all, of course, is a woodworking bench, but that's expensive.

We have given dimensions and suggested assembly techniques for the various projects shown in this book. Both can be varied. If you want to make something of a different size or in a different way—or something totally different—go ahead. Use your imagination.

BASIC TOOLS
AND HOW TO USE THEM

DRIVING TOOLS

THE HAMMER

The hammer is used to drive nails, to remove nails, and to tap pieces of wood into place before nailing. A full-sized hammer weighs 16 ounces and is 13¾ inches long. A more comfortable size for most young people to use weighs 10 ounces and is 12½ inches long.

How to start a nail

When you start a nail, hold the nail on the wood and tap it lightly with the hammer until the nail stands by itself. Then move your hand away and start hammering the nail deeper. Hold the hammer handle at the end where it feels most comfortable for you. Check that your nails go in straight. If a nail goes askew, remove it at once and start a new nail in a different place.

How to pull out a nail

A block of wood under the hammer head makes the nail easier to pull out. Hold the handle at the end. Pull it toward you with a slow, steady movement and the nail will lift out easily.

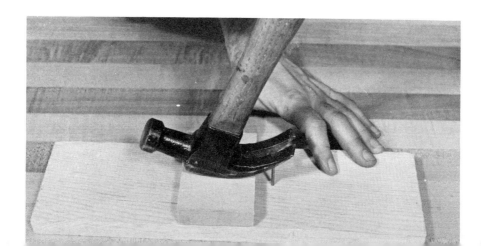

Never leave pieces of wood around that have nails sticking through them. Either pull the nails out or bend them over so that they can't hurt anyone.

How to assemble two pieces of wood

Make sure that the nails you use are not too short to hold the pieces of wood together, or so long that they will split the wood or come out the other side.

Always nail the thinner piece of wood to the thicker piece. This gives the nail more wood to sink into and to hold tight.

Be careful to place the nail correctly. If the nail is too close to the outer edge, it will stick out the side of the wood. The same thing will happen if you nail too close to the inner edge.

You can begin driving your nails on your work surface. Drive them until they just begin to come through the other side. Then put the first piece of wood carefully over the piece you are nailing into. When both pieces are exactly right, start hammering nails. But do not hammer them all the way in until you are sure they will not split the wood or come out at a wrong angle.

THE SCREWDRIVER

A screwdriver is used to drive screws into wood.

The *standard screwdriver* has a chisel-like tip to it. It is used with screws that have straight slots in their heads. The *Phillips screwdriver* is used to drive screws with cross-shaped slots in their heads.

CUTTING TOOLS

THE SAW

To cut clean and true is the first, basic skill of the wood-worker. The more you practice, the better you'll get. There are two saw categories: rip saws (top) and crosscut saws (bottom).

A *rip saw* is made to cut parallel to the grain of the wood. Its teeth are sharpened straight across the points and have a cutting action similar to that of a chisel.

A *crosscut saw* is used for cutting across the grain—sawing a board off to size. The teeth are sharpened on both sides and have a cutting action similar to that of a knife. The 20-inch crosscut saw is best for most young people. Shorter than the full-size saw adults use, it is a bit easier to handle.

How to saw

Wood to be sawed should be clamped down and marked with a pencil line. Always allow for the thickness of the saw cut (approximately $\frac{1}{16}$ inch) and saw on the waste-wood side of the line.

Using your thumb to guide the blade, start with a slow backstroke to "set" the blade. Notice the grip. Extending your index finger along the side of the handle helps to direct the stroke. The saw should now start cutting, and you can begin a steady push-pull action. The cut is actually made on the forward or push strokes. The saw should be straight and at a right angle to the wood. Keep your forearm and the saw blade in line.

It is helpful to blow away the sawdust so that you can see the pencil line as the cut is made. You should hold the piece you are sawing to prevent it from breaking off or splintering when you get near the end.

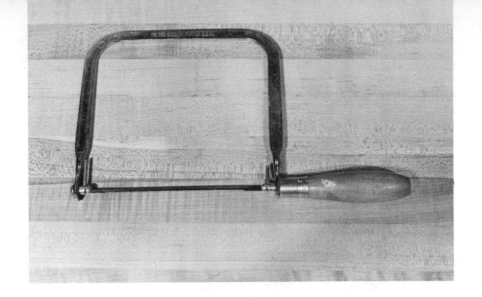

The Coping Saw

A coping saw has a thin, narrow blade held in tension. It can cut complex shapes because the slender blade can be turned within the width of the cut made. A coping blade has very fine teeth which are reversed so that they cut on the backstroke, rather than on the forestroke as most saws do. The backstroke is not as powerful as the forestroke, but it can be more precisely controlled.

The coping saw can be used to cut interior shapes. Detach the blade, thread it through a drilled hole, and reattach it for cutting inside the piece.

SHAPING TOOLS

CHISELS AND GOUGES

The *chisel* is used as a shaving tool to cut away chunks of waste and to make various joint cuts when joining two or more pieces of wood together. It can be struck with a wooden mallet or forced by hand. It has a strong blade with a handle to guide it. The wedge of its blade cuts and lifts the waste out of the way to shape and fashion wood. The wedge and the edge are the two parts of the most ancient tools: axes, adzes, and chisels.

A *gouge* cuts grooves. Its blade is rounded while the chisel is flat. There are many varieties and sizes of each and they are generally used in carving.

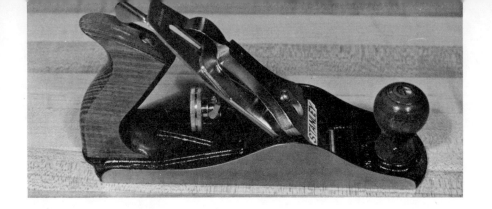

THE PLANE

A plane is a tool for shaping a flat, smooth surface.

The *smoothing plane* is one of many types of planes. It is between 8 and 12 inches long and is the plane commonly used for most purposes. Use it to smooth sides and ends of pieces, to smooth off edges, or even to make round corners. Planes work best when your work is clamped firmly in place. The plane requires pressure and elbow grease, so don't be afraid to press down with it. Try it out on a scrap piece to get the feel of it. When the cutting edge of your plane gets dull, sharpen the blade.

How to square off a block of wood

Plane one edge straight and square. Use a smoothing plane and test the corners for squareness with a try square from both sides.

9

Square one end with a try square and cut off the excess wood with a crosscut saw. Plane the end grain smooth in the direction of the unfinished edge. Take short strokes and be careful when you reach the edge of the board. A slight chamfer on this edge will prevent splitting. (A chamfer is an angle cut off along an edge.)

Measure the length desired. Mark off the surplus wood with a try square and cut off the end with a crosscut saw. Plane the end grain smooth.

Measure the width desired. Use a ruler and draw a pencil along the line. Saw off the excess wood with a rip saw and plane to the line. Test with try square both ways.

BORING TOOLS

THE DRILL

A drill is a tool for making holes in wood.

The *hand drill,* which is used for small projects, has a handle that turns a gear, a chuck to hold cutting bits or twist drills, and two knobs to help you keep the drill straight. With drill bits that fit into the chuck you can make holes up to ¼ inch in diameter.

A *countersink* is a special bit with a flaring head that makes small, cone-shaped holes or depressions in a surface. It is used most frequently to allow screw heads to fit flush with the surface of the wood.

How to insert the drill bit
To insert the drill bit (the part that makes the holes), lock the gear handle still with your thumb and turn the chuck until the three steel jaws open wide enough to hold the bit. Put the bit into the chuck as far as it will go. To tighten, keep the gear handle locked and rotate the chuck in the opposite direction as hard as you can.

How to drill a hole

Drilling by hand is not as easy as it looks. Don't press down too hard, and keep the gear handle turning at a steady rate. Always hold the drill straight or you may snap off the bit.

Drilling a $\frac{1}{4}''$ hole is done in two steps. First clamp your work in a "sandwich" between two pieces of scrap lumber. Then make a hole with a $\frac{1}{8}''$ or $\frac{11}{32}''$ bit. To remove the drill, turn the gear away from you as you pull the drill gently upward. Now finish the job by enlarging the smaller holes with a $\frac{1}{4}''$ bit.

The *brace and bit* is generally used for larger holes. Standard auger bits go from $\frac{1}{4}''$ to $1''$, increasing in size by $\frac{1}{16}''$. For larger holes you have to use an expansion bit. It has a side cutter controlled by a screw which allows you to increase or decrease the size of the hole to be cut.

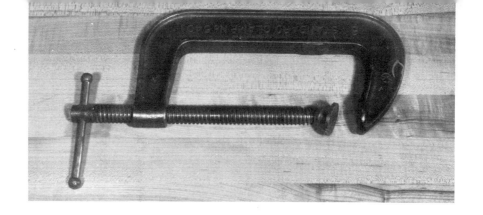

THE C-CLAMP

The C-clamp is like a third hand. If you don't have a vise, you'll need a C-clamp to hold wood steady while you're sawing, drilling or planing. The most useful sizes are the 3-inch and the 5-inch clamps.

Always protect your work with a piece of scrap wood. If you don't, the clamp will bite into the work and leave deep round marks that are impossible to get rid of.

MEASURING TOOLS

THE TRY SQUARE

The try square is an L-shaped measuring tool that helps you do accurate work. It is used to mark wood for cutting, to see if a board is warped, to check how accurately two pieces of wood have been joined together, and to check for squareness. The try square is also a handy ruler, since one leg is marked off in inches.

A special type of try square is the combination square. It is used in a similar manner, but has a sliding blade usually one foot long. One corner of the handle is usually cut off diagonally and is used to check out 45° angle cuts and joints.

How to square a board

Boards often come with ragged and unsquare ends that must be removed. To square the end of a board, hold your try square firmly against one edge and draw your line for sawing across the face of the board. Draw the line at least 1 inch from the end of the board or you'll have a hard time sawing. To check for squareness, hold the square firmly against the wood. The blade and handle of the square should fit snugly against the edge and end of the wood.

THE TAPE MEASURE

You must measure wood very carefully, or the pieces will not fit. Always double-check a measurement before you make a cut. The roll-up steel tape measure is the handiest measuring tool. It stretches as long as you need it, yet fits in your pocket. The tape measure has a steel L on the end that hooks over one end of a board, holding it in place as you take the measurement. Keep the tape straight. If it is at an angle your measurement will be off. Make your mark lightly near the edge of board.

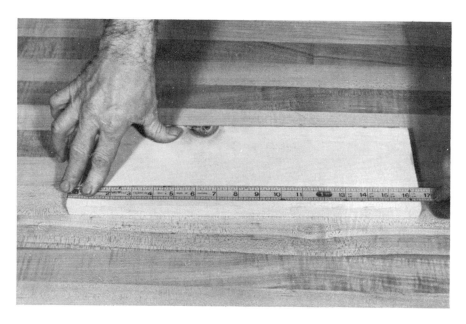

THE MITER BOX

A miter box is used to cut angles.

Some miter boxes are adjustable to any angle, but most are simple U-shaped wooden boxes with slots cut in two sides to guide a saw while cutting. A miter box can be used to cut a 45° angle (the angle that will join two boards at a 90° angle) or a "square" angle (90°). The piece to be cut is clamped or held very tightly against the side and bottom of the box. It is also a good idea to place a piece of scrap wood between the wood to be cut and the bottom of the box.

THE COMPASS AND DIVIDERS

The *compass* is used primarily to swing arcs and circles. It has two legs which are adjustable. One leg has a point at the end

which is driven into the wood to hold it securely. The second leg is fitted with a clamp that holds a pencil.

The measurement between point and pencil tip is called the radius, and the widest measurement across a circle is called the diameter.

The *dividers* are similar to the compass but have a point at the end of each leg. They can also be used to scribe circles and to step off repeated dimensions.

Tips on measuring and marking

To find the center of a piece of wood, draw lines diagonally from corner to corner. The point at which they meet will be the center.

For marking special shapes, first draw the outline of the shape on a piece of cardboard. Cut out the shape to form a template, which can then be used to trace the outline onto the wood to be cut. A plate or any circular object can be used for drawing circles or curves.

A large curve can be drawn by driving a nail a little way into the wood at each end of the curve, placing a very thin, flexible piece of wood against the nails, and bending it to the desired shape, which is then traced with a pencil.

When cutting a piece of wood into lengths, allow approximately ¹⁄₁₆″ for the thickness of the saw blade.

FASTENINGS

NAILS

The *common nail* has a large, flat head which is easy to hit with a hammer. But the nailhead will show after the nail is driven in. Use common nails when it doesn't matter if the nailheads show or when you plan to paint over them.

The *finishing nail* and *brad* have much smaller heads. They can be recessed into the wood with a round tapered tool called a "nail set" so that the head does not show as much. To hide the nailhead, fill in the hole left by the nail with plastic wood in the same color you intend to finish the project. Use either finishing nails or brads for finer work or for projects that you will stain or shellac.

Woodworkers and hardware dealers don't call nails 2-inch or 3-inch nails but rather 6-penny or 8-penny nails. Years ago, you bought a hundred nails for four pennies or six pennies or eight pennies, depending on the size. Naturally the smaller nails cost fewer pennies. We still talk of nail sizes in this way, even though you now buy nails by the pound or by the box.

GLUE

The strength of glue depends on the bond between its own substance and the shallow layer of wood it penetrates. It is important then that the surfaces to be joined are clean.

How to glue

Spread glue thoroughly over both surfaces of the wood to be joined. Squeeze the glue from the container in a thin, steady stream. Spread the glue with a scrap of wood.

Clamps should be used to squeeze the pieces of wood together. This will insure a more perfect bond between pieces as the glue dries. Do not use too much glue. If some oozes out when you clamp the pieces together, wipe it off. If you let it dry, it will spoil your finish.

Types of glue

Elmer's glue is a good all-purpose glue. For outside projects you must use waterproof glue.

Contact cement is usually a rubber-based adhesive and is used for sticking on a veneer or plastic-based surface such as Formica. It is spread on both surfaces and allowed to dry before putting the surfaces together. Make sure you position pieces before you join them, because they will not move after they have touched.

SCREWS

A screw is a threaded piece of metal which is designed to pull two pieces of wood together. It has greater holding power than a nail.

Wood screws are measured by the diameter of their shank (given in a number between 0 and 16) and by their length in inches. Bronze or brass screws are used decoratively, or when there is a possibility of dampness, because they will not corrode or rust. Steel screws are used for heavy-duty work. Screw heads come in many shapes and each has a specific purpose. The basic shapes are oval-head, round-head, and flat-head.

Joining wood together with screws requires preparatory holes to be drilled in the various pieces to be joined in order to avoid splitting the wood. This is especially important when hard woods are used, because there is little give in the grain.

In all cases at least two holes should be drilled. They are the shank hole and the pilot hole. The shank hole is drilled to the same size as the shank diameter of the screw. The screw should fit snugly in this hole.

The pilot hole should be drilled into the base piece to be joined. It is made slightly smaller than the diameter of the screw thread. This will allow the threads to bite into the wood easily and will draw the two pieces of wood together.

When more than two pieces are being joined together, the pilot hole should be drilled only in the base piece. Shank holes should be drilled in the other pieces. This will allow all pieces to be drawn together tightly.

If flat-head or oval-head screws are used, a countersunk hole should be drilled into the shank hole. This will allow the tapered part of the screw head to fit snugly into the wood. It will also allow flat-head screws to be flush with the surface of the wood.

DOWELS

A dowel is a wooden pin used to join pieces of wood. The principle of the dowel is simple. The pieces of wood to be joined are placed together and a common hole is drilled through them. The dowel (cut from a length of dowel rod) is fitted snugly into the hole and is fastened by glue. Glue should also be applied to the surfaces being joined. The joined pieces should be clamped together until the glue is dry to insure a snug fit.

WOOD

Woods are groups in two broad categories: softwoods and hardwoods. Examples of softwoods are pine, fir, spruce, and hemlock. Hardwoods, such as maple, oak, and walnut, are generally much more expensive and tend to be more difficult to work.

All lumber has a grain, which is a pattern caused by the trees' growth. In boards the grain runs lengthwise. This is referred to as edge grain. The pattern of fibers showing at either end of a board is called end grain.

Lumber is sold in lengths of even-numbered feet, usually beginning with 4 feet. After that you can buy boards that are 6, 8, 10 . . . feet—all the way to 18 feet long. Longer lengths can be obtained by special orders. When you build something, you have to figure out how many feet you actually need and then buy the next larger even-numbered length. If you need 8½ feet, you have to buy 10 feet.

The size of a piece of lumber is indicated in inches. The first numeral tells the thickness of the board, the second tells its width. Thus a 1"×8" board ("one by eight") is 1 inch thick by 8 inches wide. Actually, although a board is called 1"×8", it really measures less, because there is an amount of wood lost when the board is planed. A so-called 1″ board is closer to ¾ inch in thickness. And a so-called 8″ width is closer to 7½ inches. A good rule to follow to figure actual size is to subtract ¼ inch from the thickness and ½ inch from the width.

Be choosy when you go to buy lumber. Look through the pile until you find what you want.

Boards with too many knots should be avoided. Knots in general are very hard to cut through and impossible to nail. If there are knots, they should be tight or firm; large loose knots should be avoided, because they usually fall out.

Make sure the boards are not warped and that the ends of the boards are not cracked or split.

Be sure the wood has been well seasoned by either kiln drying or natural drying. This can be determined by asking the salesperson.

WOOD FINISHING

Finishing (or painting) a project is just as important as making it. Stain, varnish, shellac, lacquer, and paint are finishes which seal and protect the wood and make the article look more attractive. Raw or unfinished wood quickly becomes dirty and hard to clean.

Staining is easiest, because you just brush the stain on and that's it. Adding a few coats of wax will deepen the natural grain of the wood. The results will be worth the extra effort.

Applying a few coats of a clear finish, such as varnish, shellac, or lacquer, will serve many purposes. First, the finish brings out the natural beauty of the wood grain. Second, it seals the wood against moisture and therefore helps prevent splitting and warping. Third, it deepens the color of stains. And, fourth it helps protect the wood surface. Allow each coat of the finish to dry overnight before applying additional coats. Rubbing each coat down with fine steel wool after it dries will help eliminate dust specks and air bubbles, and will result in a smoother finish.

Painting takes the most time and most effort. First you should cover any knots with white shellac. Then use a white undercoat and finally two coats of the paint. Each coat must be allowed to dry thoroughly before applying the next.

How you finish a project depends on how you want the job to look. There are so many types of varnish and paint that it will pay you to consult a specialist.

Helpful hints

Before you start finishing, be sure you have everything you need: old newspapers, empty cans or cut-down milk cartons to hold stain or paint, brushes, paint stirrers, rags to wipe up spills, and some old clothes.

Whenever possible, try to buy the exact amount of paint for the job, as leftover paint will deteriorate with time.

Make sure the wood surface is smooth, clean, and dry. Put the paint on evenly and do not overload the brush.

Do your sanding away from where you do your painting, as the dust will stick to wet paint and make a rough surface. Outside is best.

Clean all brushes immediately after use with the proper solvent. Brushes used to apply shellac must be cleaned with alcohol. Lacquer thinner must be used to clean brushes used to apply lacquer-based finishes. Brushes used to apply oil-based paints, varnishes, and similar finishes must be cleaned in turpentine, benzine, or paint thinner. In all cases the brush should be washed with soap and warm water to remove any residue left from the thinner. It is a good practice to hang the brushes to dry with the hairs pointing down.

When you are through, put covers on all cans. Make sure they are tight so that air cannot enter and dry up the contents. Store them away from fires and warm places.

Basic procedures

Before assembling pieces, sand each piece of the project on all faces, edges, and ends with the grain until smooth. Use No. 1½ and No. 2 sandpaper.

After the project is assembled, scrape off any excess glue and erase all pencil marks.

Sand the entire project with the grain, using No. 1 and No. 0 (fine) sandpaper until it is smooth.

If you plan to paint, a prime or basic coat of paint should be applied to the wood. Allow the paint to dry overnight. Apply the first coat of paint and allow it to dry overnight. Give the object a second coat if necessary. After the first coat is dry, sand it down lightly to remove rough spots.

If you plan to stain the project, apply the stain with a rag or brush against the grain of the wood. Allow 15 minutes for penetration. Then rub the surface down with a rag in the direction of the grain.

To deepen the color of the stain, a clear finish such as shellac, lacquer, or varnish can be applied. At least two or three coats should be applied to provide a good finish. Allow at least 4 hours drying time, and rub the surface down with steel wool between each coat and after the final coat. Then rub down with furniture paste wax to bring up the luster.

PROJECTS

BASEBALL GAME

Materials:
One 6"×12"×¾" board
One ½"×3½"×¾" piece of plywood
Sandpaper
One No. 6×1" round-head brass screw
Clear finish or wax
One ³⁄₁₆" length of plastic tubing

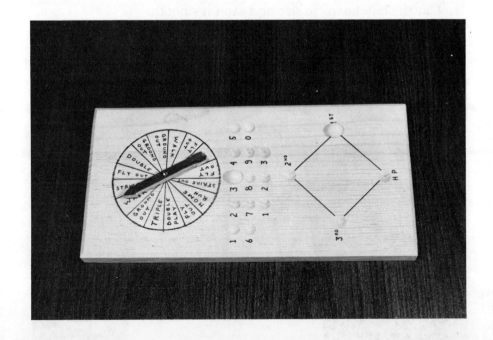

Description:

With this easy-to-make baseball game you can play an entire season of games, including playoffs and world series. You merely spin the arrow and keep track of the action with marbles placed in countersunk holes representing runs scored, men on base, and outs made in each inning. Innings played and total runs scored can be recorded on a regular baseball score card.

Procedure:

1. Cut the baseboard to size and sand it smooth.
2. The playing circle has sixteen sections and will be laid out as follows:

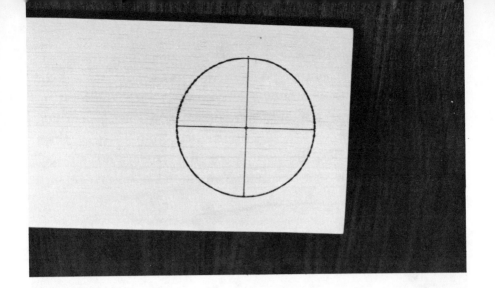

a) Measure in 3 inches from one side and 3 inches from one end to find the center of the scoring circle. Set a compass for a 2-inch radius and scribe a circle. Darken in the circle line with a felt-tipped pen.

b) Using a try square and a felt-tipped pen, draw lines through the center of the circle perpendicular to the end and the side of the board. This will divide the circle into four sections.

c) To divide each of the four sections into four equal parts, set the ends of the compass ¾ inch apart. Place the compass point where one of the cross lines intersects the circle and mark a point on the circle ¾ inch away.

31

Then move the compass point to your new mark and measure off another point ¾ inch farther on around the circle. Continue stepping off points ¾ inch apart in this way halfway around the circle. Now, using a ruler, draw a line with a felt-tipped pen from each of these points through the center of the circle and straight across to the opposite side. You should now have sixteen sections.

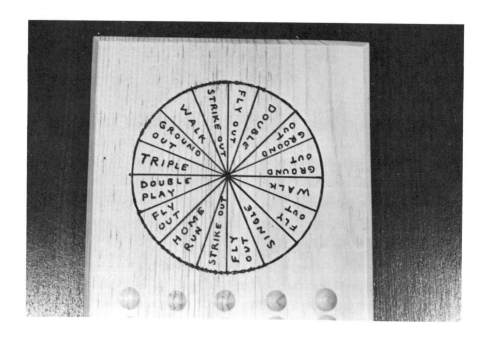

d) Each of these sections will represent a play. You can letter in any combination of plays you wish with a felt-tipped pen. The board shown includes the following plays: One single, one double, one triple, one home run, two walks, two strike-outs, three ground-outs, four fly-outs, and one double play (count as one out if no one is on base). Space out the hits and walks so that they are not next to each other.

3. Lay out the diamond as follows:

    a) Cut out a 2-inch square of cardboard. Find the center of the width of the board and measure in on this line 1 inch from the end opposite the scoring circle. Place the try square on this line and slip the cardboard diamond under it so that the two opposite corners line up with the center line.

    b) Remove the try square and trace the cardboard diamond with the felt-tipped pen.

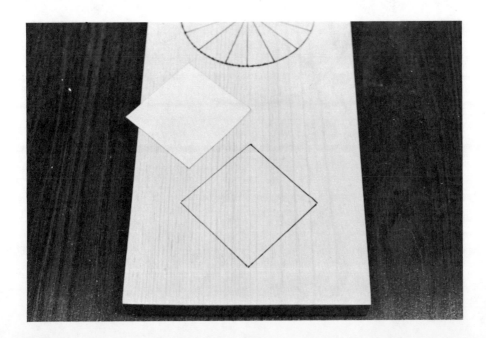

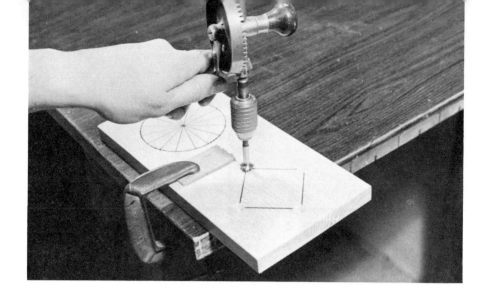

c) Drill a countersunk hole at each point of the diamond to represent the four bases. With the felt-tipped pen, label the holes HP, 1st, 2nd, and 3rd. Marbles placed in these holes will be used to keep track of the players on base.

4. To keep track of the runs scored and outs made in an inning, countersink ten holes for runs and three holes for outs. To do this, draw three light pencil lines across the board equally spaced between the diamond and the circle.

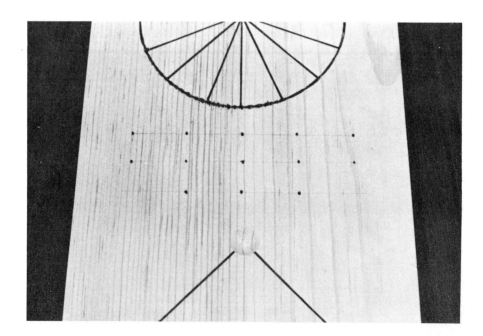

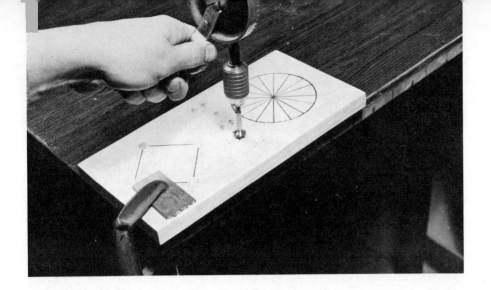

On two of the lines measure in from one edge 1 inch and make five marks 1 inch apart. On the third line measure in from the edge 2 inches and make three marks 1 inch apart. Drill countersunk holes at each of the marks. Erase the pencil lines and letter in 1 to 10 for the runs, and 1 to 3 for the outs.

5. Chamfer or round the top edges and ends with a file. To finish the board, apply a clear lacquer, shellac, or varnish, or simply wax.

6. Draw an arrow on the plywood and drill a ⅛-inch hole at the center point for the screw which holds the arrow to the board to pass through. Cut out the shape of the arrow with a coping saw and sand all sides of the arrow.

7. Drill a ⅟₁₆-inch pilot hole at the center of the circle. Insert the No. 6×1″ brass screw through the hole in the arrow. Place a small piece of plastic tubing around the screw between the board and the arrow to prevent friction when spinning the arrow.

8. Fasten the screw to the baseboard.

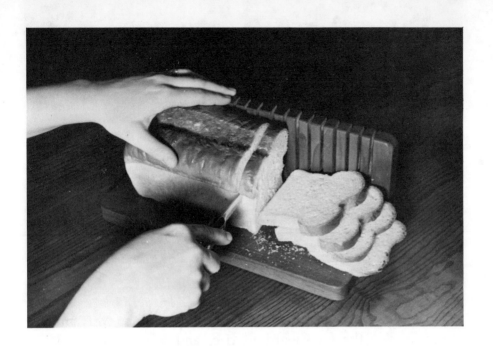

BREAD SLICING BOARD

Materials:
One 7″×14″×¾″ walnut or cherry board
Two 6¾″×7″×¾″ walnut or cherry boards
Four No. 8×2″ flat-head screws
Sandpaper
Vegetable oil

Description:
This bread slicing board has narrow slots in the backboard which provide a guide for the knife when slicing whole loaves of bread. This will help in cutting slices of bread of even thickness. A close-grained hardwood such as walnut or cherry should be used, as these woods will stand up better to the cutting action of the knife. The slots cut into the backboards must be made with the grain. This will give the resulting narrow strips of wood between the slots greater strength and stiffness.

Procedure:

1. Cut the large piece for the baseboard and two smaller pieces for the backboard to size, and sand smooth. (It is extremely difficult to find hardwoods in widths greater than 8 or 10 inches. Therefore, two pieces 7 inches wide are used to make the backboard since the grain must run in the 6¾-inch direction.)

2. Measure in 2 inches from the right side of one backboard piece, and 2 inches from the left side of the other backboard piece. From these marks measure off every ½ inch toward the opposite side on each backboard. Draw parallel lines along these marks with a try square from the top end grain to within ¾ inch of the bottom end grain.

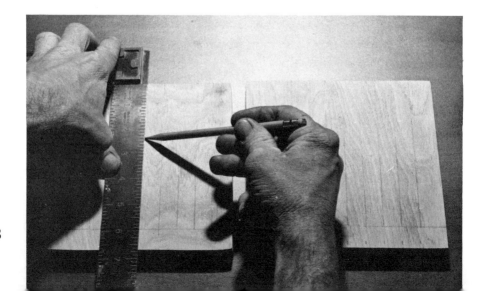

3. Clamp the boards to the worktable and cut along each line to the end of the drawn line with a handsaw. Sand the rough edges smooth.

4. Drill two shank holes into each backboard ½ inch in from each end and ⅜ inch from the bottom edge. Countersink each hole ⅛ inch deep.

5. Drill pilot holes into the edge of the baseboard to match the shank holes in the backboards, allowing for ¹⁄₁₆ inch space between the backboards.
6. Assemble the baseboard and backboards and fasten them together with No. 8×2″ flat-head screws.
7. Rub the surface down with vegetable oil.

CHOPPING BOARD

Materials:
One 10"×15"×¾" walnut or cherry board
Two 3"×6"×¾" walnut or cherry legs
Four No. 8×1½" flat-head screws
Sandpaper
Vegetable oil

Description:
This chopping board has legs which raise it, so that a bowl can be placed underneath into which foods can be scraped as they are cut. Hardwood should be used to withstand the cutting action of the knife.

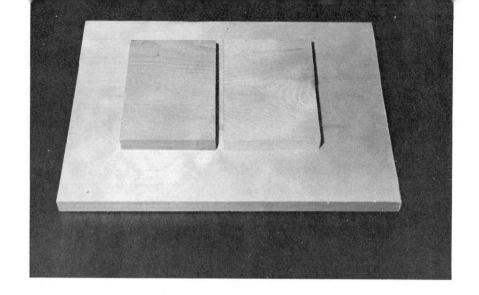

Procedure:

1. Cut the board and legs to overall size and sand them smooth.
2. Find the center of the board along one end and draw a semicircle 6 inches in diameter. Round off each corner of the board using a 2-inch radius. Clamp the board to your worktable and cut out the shape with a coping saw.

3. Lay out the shape of the legs as shown. Clamp the wood to the worktable and cut out the shape with the coping saw. Round off the edges with the file and sand all surfaces smooth.

4. Drill two shank holes into the straight crosspiece of each leg with a hand drill.

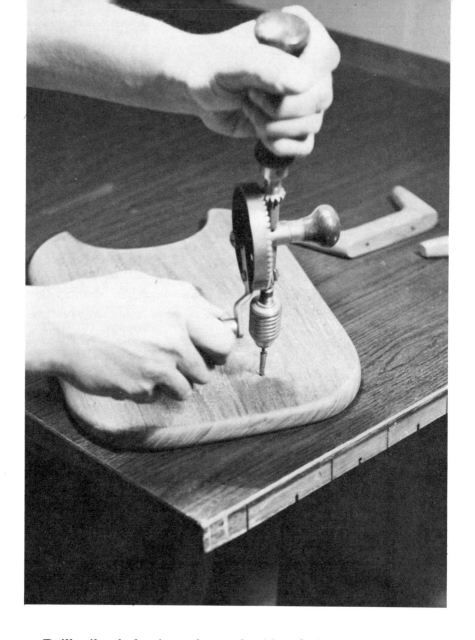

5. Drill pilot holes into the underside of the board to match the shank holes in the legs. Be careful not to drill through the top surface of the board. Place a piece of tape on the drill bit ½ inch from the point as a guide.

6. Assemble the board and the legs and fasten them together with No. 8×1½" flat-head screws. Rub the board down with vegetable oil.

PERPETUAL CALENDAR

Materials:

One 10″×14″×¾″ pine board
Seventy-two 1″ brass disks
Forty-three No. 4×¾″ round-head brass screws
Sandpaper
Stain

Description:

The brass disks used in this calendar have numbers painted on them and are hung on small brass screws. The holes in the disks are slightly larger than the screw heads. This makes it possible to move the disks around according to the month and year. The result is a calendar that can be used for a lifetime.

Procedure:

1. Cut the board to size and lay out the screw holes and shape according to the diagram.

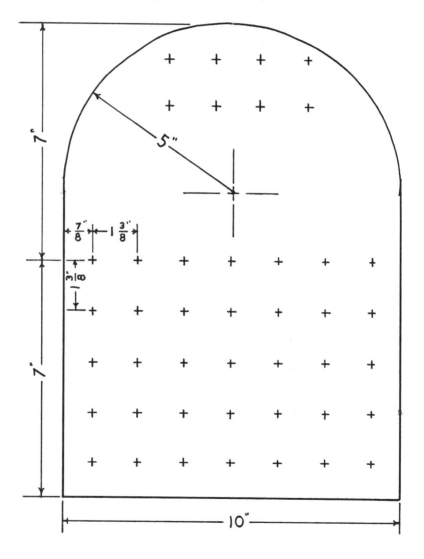

2. Clamp the wood to your worktable and drill pilot holes with a ¹⁄₁₆″ bit ¼-inch deep at the marks laid out.

3. Cut out the shape of the board with a coping saw. Sand the face and edges smooth, and stain the board.

NUMBER OF DAYS IN EACH MONTH
Jan. 31 Feb. 28 March 31 April 30 May 31 June 30
July 31 Aug. 31 Sept. 30 Oct. 31 Nov. 30 Dec. 31

4. Paint the first letter of each day of the week ½ inch above the top row of pilot holes made for the thirty-one days of the month. You may also wish to paint in other information in the space left between the year and the days of the month as was done in this project.

5. Fasten the ¾″ brass screws in the pilot holes. Leave the heads of each screw ⅛ inch above the face of the wood. This will allow the holes in the disks to slip over the screw head and hang on the screw shanks.

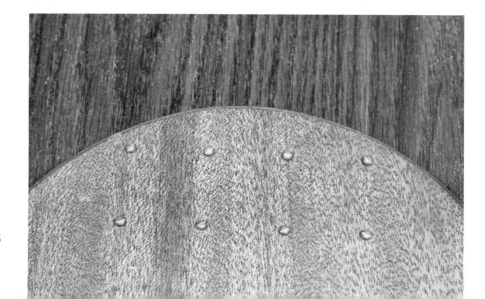

6. The brass disks measure 1 inch in diameter by 1/16 inch thick and can be purchased in a hardware store. You will need thirty-one disks, to be numbered 1 through 31, for the days of the month. For the years you will need twenty-two disks. Two disks are used for the first two digits of the century—1 and 9 (you can also paint a 2 and 0 on the backs to represent the next century). The remaining twenty disks will be used to represent the last two digits of the decade and year; you will need two sets of numbers from 1 to 0. For the months of the year you will need nineteen disks— one for each letter of the alphabet except H, I, K, Q, W, X, and Z. With these disks you can assemble the first three or four letters of each month. The letters and numerals can be painted on the disks with enamel paint; or you can use adhesive letters or Pres-Type, which can be purchased in any artists' supply store.

7. Apply a clear finish.

BRACKET AND SHELF

Materials:

One 7"×9"×1½" pine board
One 10"×10"×¾" pine board
One screw hanger
Two No. 8×¾" flat-head screws
One No. 8×1" flat-head screw
Three 1½" brads
Stain

Description:

The bracket and shelf shown was made to hang on a beam between large picture windows. It is ideal for holding potted plants and at the same time will not block the view through the windows. You can, of course, hang it anywhere else you like.

The screw hanger, which you can buy at the lumberyard or a hardware store, is fitted into a recessed area on the back of the bracket. It consists of a strip of metal with a keyhole-shaped or figure-8 slot at one end and two holes for screws to attach it to the bracket. The bottom end of the figure 8 is large enough to fit over the head of a screw driven into the beam or wall where you want to hang the shelf. Then the assembly slips down so that the smaller top end of the figure 8 is resting on the shank of the screw. The head of the screw is larger than the small end of the figure 8 and will hold the bracket in place against the beam. By this recessed screwhanger device, the bracket and shelf hang on the beam without any visible means of support.

Procedure:

1. Cut the boards for the bracket and shelf to overall size. Both pieces can be given an antique look by hammering dents in the wood, or they can be sanded smooth.

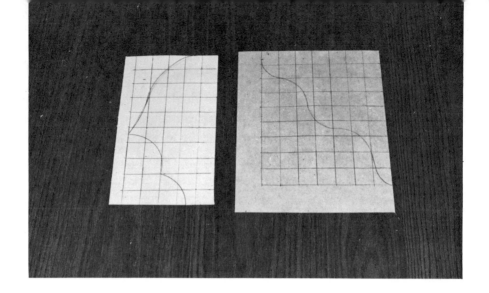

2. Rule grids of 1-inch squares—one 5 by 10 inches and one 7 by 9 inches—on pieces of thin cardboard. Draw half the shape of the shelf onto the 5″×10″ grid, and the entire shape of the bracket onto the 7″×9″ grid. Cut out each shape with scissors.

3. Place the straight edge of the shelf pattern onto the center line of the 10″×10″ piece of wood. Trace the pattern onto one half of the wood; then flip the pattern over and trace it onto the second half to complete the design.

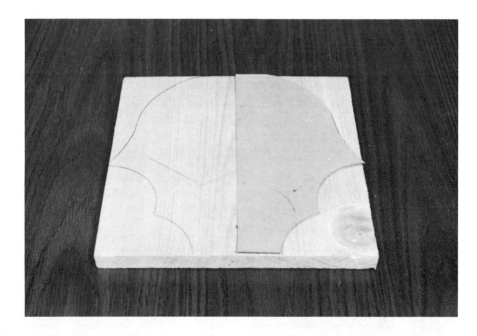

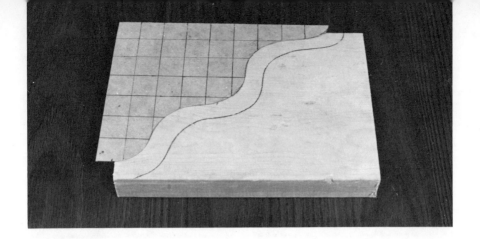

4. Place the bracket pattern onto the 7″×9″ piece of wood and trace the entire design. The grain should be running parallel to the 9-inch side.
5. Clamp each piece of wood to your worktable and cut out the shapes with a coping saw.

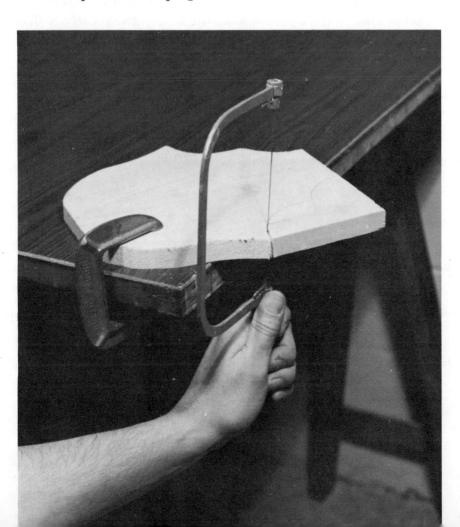

6. Center the screw hanger on the back of the bracket ½ inch below the top edge, and trace the overall shape of the hanger. Cut a recess into the bracket with a chisel, as deep as the thickness of the screw hanger.

7. Place the screw hanger into the recess (making sure the small end of the figure-8 slot will be toward the top), and mark a point on the wood at the center of the figure 8.

Drill a hole into the wood at this point large enough to match the long dimension of the figure 8 and ½ inch deep. Fasten the screw hanger to the bracket with two No. 8×¾″ flat-head screws.

8. Stain the shelf and bracket. Center the shelf onto the top edge of the bracket, and nail them together with 1½″ brads.

9. Drive a No. 8×1″ round-head screw into the window beam. Leave the head of the screw extending about ¼ inch and hang the screw hanger onto the shank of the screw.

ADJUSTABLE BOOK RACK

Materials:
Two 7″×7″×¾″ pine boards
Two 9″×12″×¾″ pine boards
Eight No. 8×2″ flat-head screws
Sandpaper
Stain or paint

Description:
Adjustable book racks have an obvious advantage over fixed book racks. They can be enlarged or reduced, within limits, as books are added or removed, and will still hold the remaining books in an upright position. Book racks are generally placed on a desk to hold those books most frequently used so that they are readily available when needed.

Procedure:

1. Cut all pieces to overall size and sand smooth.
2. Lay out the base pieces on the 9″×12″ boards—one of them in the shape of a square-bottomed U and one in the shape of a T. Rule two lines 2 inches in from each edge 9 inches long on each base with a try square. Then rule lines perpendicular to the 9-inch lines to form the base of the U and the stem of the T.

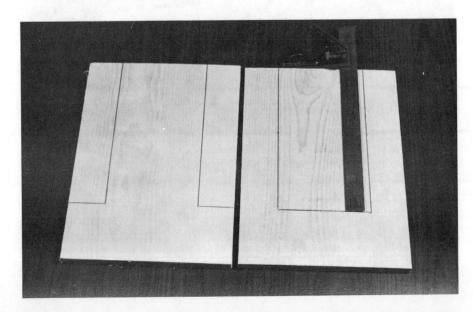

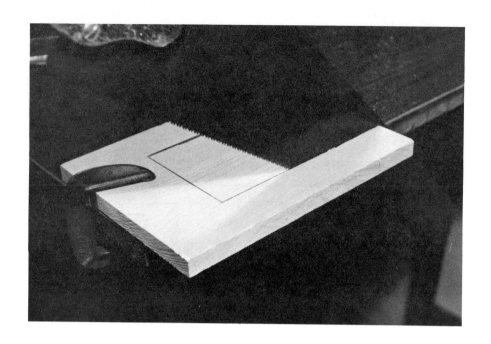

3. Clamp the U-shaped base to the worktable. Cut along each 9-inch line with a handsaw, stopping at the base of the U.
4. Insert a coping saw into one of these cuts and saw along the base of the U.

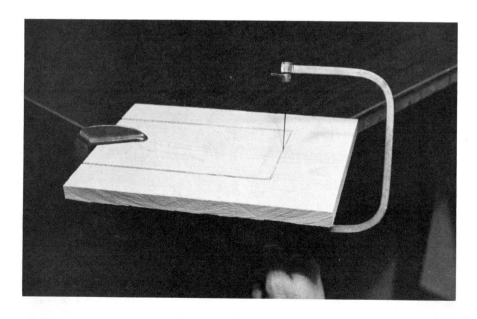

5. Clamp the T-shaped base to the worktable and make four cuts to form the T.
6. The two bases should fit perfectly into each other. File and sand the rough edges smooth.

7. Lay out the pattern of the upright ends by finding the center point of one end of each 7″×7″ piece. Measure down from this end 2 inches along each edge of both pieces. Rule two diagonal lines to connect the three points.

8. Clamp each piece to the worktable and cut out each shape with the handsaw.

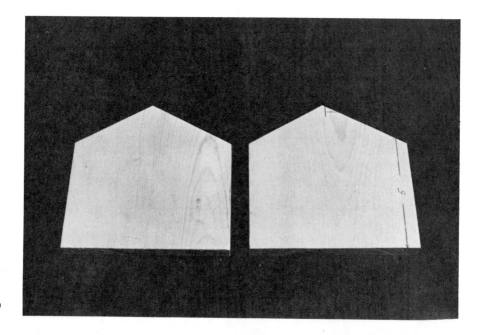

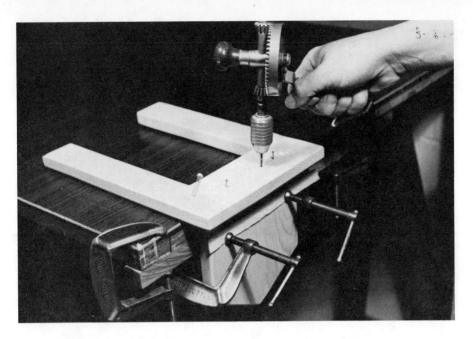

9. Drill four shank holes evenly spaced into each base so that the upright ends will be centered on the 3"×9" sections of the bases. Drill pilot holes into the end grain of the upright ends to match the shank holes in the bases.

10. Countersink the shank holes in each base deep enough so that the heads of the screws will be recessed slightly below the bottom face of the bases.

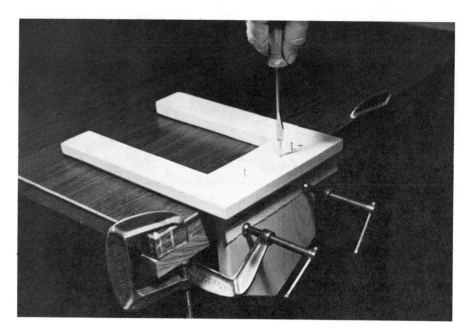

11. Assemble and fasten the bases and the upright ends together with No. 8×2″ flat-head screws. Finish with stain or paint.

PLANTER WITH TILES

Materials:

Two 8″×8″×¾″ walnut boards
Two 8″×10½″×¾″ walnut boards
One 8″×8″×¾″ pine board
Two ceramic tiles 8″×8″×½″
Twenty-four 2″ handwrought nails
Glue
Sandpaper
Stain

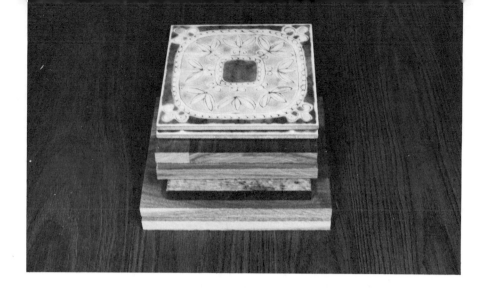

Description:

Wood and ceramic materials such as tiles are natural partners because each enhances the beauty of the other. Planters which mix these two materials add to the beauty of plants since all three are natural products of the earth.

Procedure:

1. Cut all pieces to finished size and sand smooth.
2. Drill shank holes evenly spaced into the 8″×10½″ boards (which will form the two ends of the planter) ⅞ inch in

from each end-grain edge, and ⅜ inch from the bottom edge. Four holes along each of the three edges will be enough. Drill pilot holes into the end grain of the two 8″×8″ walnut boards (the front and back sides) and into the edge grain of the pine board (the bottom) to match the shank holes.

3. Assemble the four sides and the bottom, and fasten them together with the handwrought nails. The two 8″×8″ sides will be recessed ½ inch to allow for the ½-inch thickness of the tiles. Stain or wax.

4. Apply an all-purpose glue to the backs of the tiles.

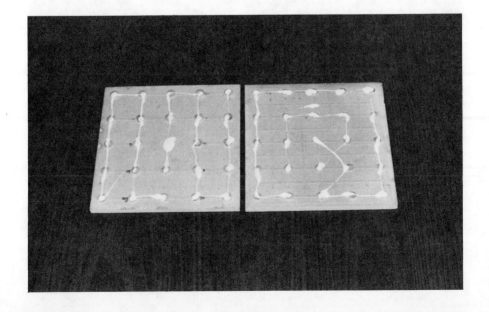

5. Position the tiles onto the 8″×8″ sides and press firmly. Allow two hours to dry.

6. Place a potted plant in the planter. If you wish to put soil directly into the planter, paint the insides with three or four coats of marine polyurethane paint.

ECOLOGY BOX

Materials:

Two 2″×8½″×¾″ pine boards
Two 2″×10″×¾″ pine boards
Four ¼″×10″×¾″ pine boards
Ten ½″×2″ pine boards—one of each of the following lengths:
A=1″, B=2½″, C=6″, D=2″, E=2″, F=8½″, G=4½″, H=3″,
I=6″, J=1″
One 10″×10″×⅛″ piece of clear Plexiglas
One 10″×10″×¼″ piece of plywood or Masonite
Eight 2″ handwrought nails
¾″ brads
1½″ brads
Eight No. 6×1″ round-head screws
Sandpaper
Clear finish

Description:

The enjoyable thing about making ecology boxes is the unlimited variety of shapes and sizes that can be made, and of materials that can be housed in each compartment. This box includes beans, macaroni, lentils, peas, and weeds. It was made entirely from scraps of wood found around the shop. Never throw away scrap materials since you can always find something to make with a little imagination.

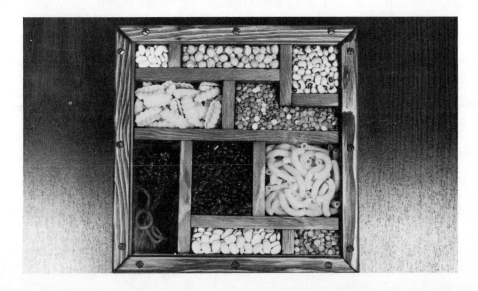

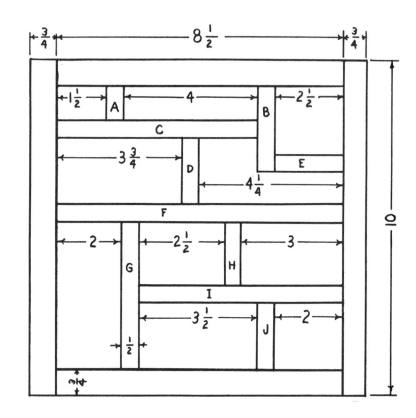

CODE
A = 1"
B = 2½"
C = 6"
D = 2"
E = 2"
F = 8½"
G = 4½"
H = 3"
I = 6"
J = 1"

Procedure:

1. Follow the diagram (or make up your own) and cut all pieces to size. Sand all showing surfaces smooth.

2. Drill shank holes in the 2"×10" boards ⅜ inch in from each end and 1 inch apart. Drill pilot holes into the ends of the 2"×8½"×¾" boards to match the shank holes.

3. Assemble the four sides and fasten them together with 2″ handwrought nails. Stain all showing surfaces.

4. Fasten the plywood or Masonite to the bottom of the box with ¾″ brads.

5. Assemble the interior partitions in a manner that will allow for easy nailing. Fasten together with 1½" brads. Use a try square to ensure square joining of each piece.
6. Place the interior section into the box. Use the try square to ensure a square fit of the partitions to the sides of the box.

7. Fasten all partitions that touch the sides of the box with
   1½" brads.
8. To make the frame, miter the ends of each of the ¼-inch-
   thick strips at a 45° angle. File and sand the edges of the
   frame round.

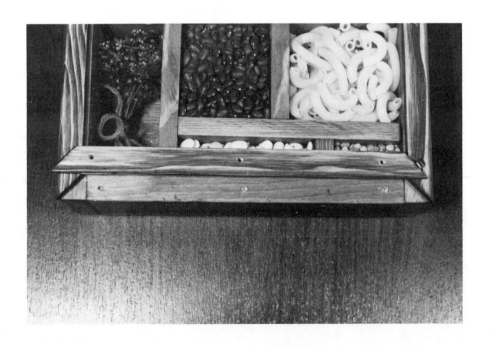

9. Assemble the Plexiglas cover and the frame. Drill shank holes through the frame and Plexiglas and pilot holes into the top edges of the box to match the shank holes. Fill the compartments and fasten the frame and Plexiglas to the box with No. 6×1″ round-head screws. A clear finish such as lacquer, varnish, or shellac can be applied to the sides and frame if desired. Allow four hours for drying and rub down with steel wool and wax. Polish with a soft cloth.

COFFEE CUP RACK

Materials:

Two 5″×18″×¾″ pine boards
Two 5″×22¼″×¾″ pine boards
Three 5″×16½″×¾″ pine boards
Ten 5″×5″×¾″ pine boards
One 18″×23¾″×¼″ piece of plywood or Masonite
Twelve 2″ handwrought nails
1½″ brads
¾″ brads
Sandpaper
Stain

Description:

What better way to store coffee mugs than in a rack that says
"COFFEE"? The letters incorporated in this design set the
rack apart from other shelf units made to hold mugs. You
can, of course, replace the letters with cutouts of geometric
shapes, leaf or flower motifs, snowflake designs, or any other
pattern you like. You can also design your own racks or shelf
units incorporating the same principles, to hold knickknacks,
utensils, small framed pictures, or anything else that comes to
mind.

Procedure:

1. Cut all pieces to size and sand smooth.
2. Drill shank holes into the 5″×18″ boards (the sides of the rack) ⅜ inch from the ends and 2 inches apart. Drill pilot holes into the ends of the 5″×22¼″ boards (the top and bottom) to match the shank holes.

3. Assemble the sides and the top and bottom, and fasten them together with 2″ handwrought nails. Stain all showing surfaces.

4. Assemble the three 5″×16½″ vertical partitions and four 5″×5″ pieces as shelves, and fasten them together with 1½″ brads. The first and third shelves are placed 5 inches from the bottom of the partitions. The second and fourth shelves are placed 5 inches from the tops of the partitions. Stain all pieces before assembly.

5. Assemble the sides and interior section and fasten together with 1½" brads.
6. Fasten the plywood or Masonite to the back of the rack with ¾" brads.

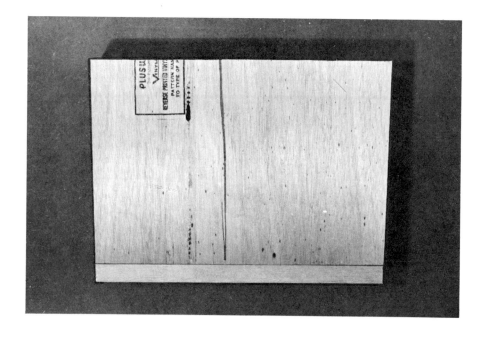

7. Lay out one letter of the word COFFEE on each of the remaining six 5″×5″ blocks. Block letters 1 inch wide were used, but you can, of course, adapt the same principle to any style letter you like.

8. Clamp each block to the worktable and cut out the letters with a coping saw. To cut out the center of the letter O, drill a pilot hole, insert the coping saw blade, and cut. Sand smooth and wax all surfaces that will show.

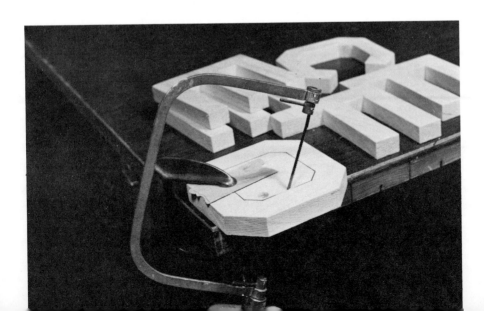

9. Assemble the letters in the proper sections as shown in the photograph of the finished project. Fasten to the partitions and the sides of the box with 1½″ brads. Store or hang in an appropriate place, and place mugs on the shelves.

SHOESHINE BOX

Materials:

Two 9″×10″×¾″ pine boards
Three 3½″×17″×¾″ pine boards
One 3½″×7″×¾″ pine board
One ½″×3½″×¾″ pine board
One 8¼″×15½″×¾″ pine board
One 10″×15½″×¾″ pine board
2″ handwrought nails
1¼″ brads
Sandpaper
Stain or paint

Description:

A shoeshine box is a useful item to have around the house—particularly since most of us never know where to store our shoe-cleaning materials. This box has a partition down the middle to separate the black and brown polishes and brushes. The use of attractive hardware, such as handwrought nails, makes a simple project more interesting.

Procedure:

1. Cut all pieces to size and sand smooth.
2. Lay out the pattern of the shoe rest directly onto the 3½"×7" board. Use a compass to draw a 3½-inch radius at the front of the shoe rest. Taper the sides toward the back slightly.

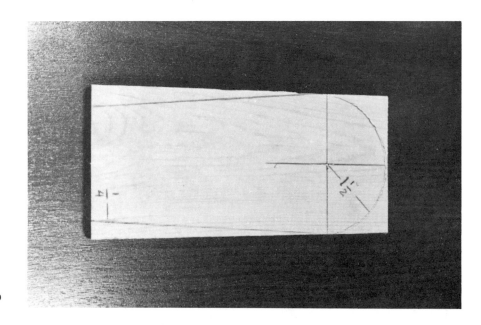

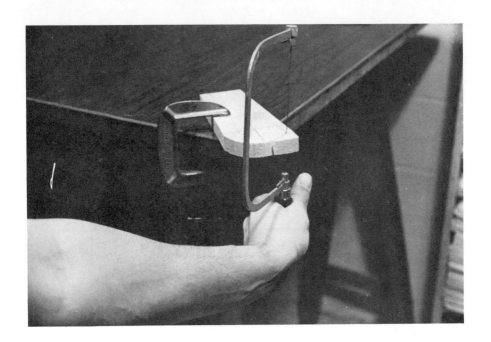

3. Clamp the wood to your worktable and cut out the shape of the shoe rest with a coping saw. Sand the sawed surfaces smooth.

4. Put the $\frac{1}{2}"\times3\frac{1}{2}"\times\frac{3}{4}"$ block as a bracket under the front of the shoe rest, and center them on top of one of the $3\frac{1}{2}"\times17"$ boards. Nail the bracket to the board, and then nail the shoe rest to the bracket and the board, using $1\frac{1}{4}"$ brads.

5. Mark a point on the edge of a piece of cardboard 3¼ inches from one corner. Mark another point on the edge perpendicular to the first edge 5½ inches from the corner. Draw a smooth curve between these two points and cut out along the line. Use this curve as a pattern to lay out the end pieces for the box on the two 9″×10″ boards as shown in the pictures. The long side of the curve runs along the 9-inch sides of the boards, and the short side of the curve lies on each end of the 10-inch sides.

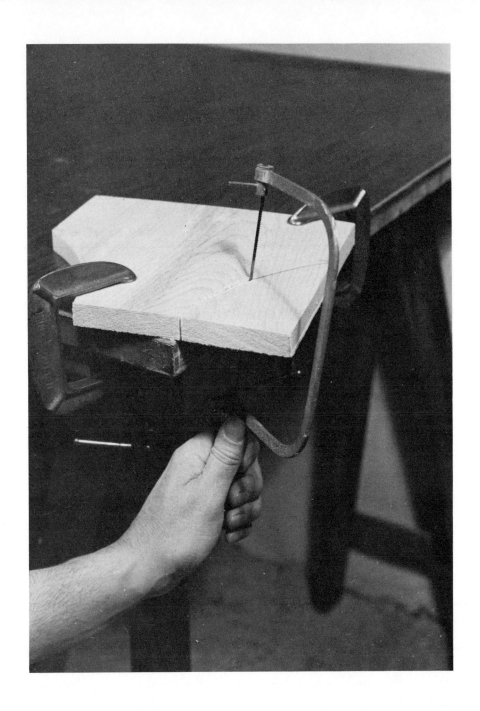

6. Clamp each end piece to the worktable and cut out the curves with a coping saw. Sand the sawed edges smooth.

7. Drill shank holes into the end, top, and side pieces, and pilot holes to match into the edges of the $8\frac{1}{4}''\times 15\frac{1}{2}''$ center partition, the $10''\times 15\frac{1}{2}''$ bottom piece, and the end pieces.

8. Assemble the end pieces to the bottom and partition and fasten them together with 2" handwrought nails. Assemble the top and sides to the end pieces and fasten them also with handwrought nails. Finish with a stain, clear finish, or colored paint.

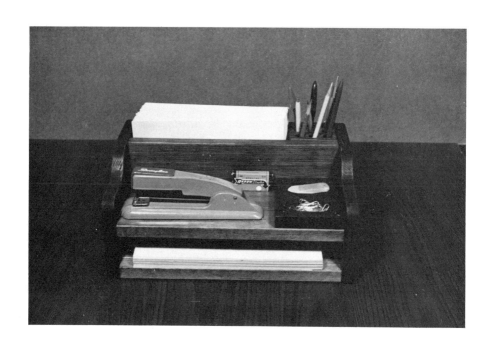

DESK ORGANIZER

Materials:

Two 9"×13"×¾" pine boards
Two 6½"×9"×¾" pine boards
One 3"×13"×¾" pine board
One 3"×3"×¾" pine board
One 4"×5¼"×¾" pine board
One 6½"×14½"×¼" plywood board
2" handwrought nails
1¼" brads
¾" brads
Sandpaper
Stain and clear lacquer

Description:

Desk organizers can be very helpful in storing items together. This particular organizer was designed to store writing materials in one convenient place.

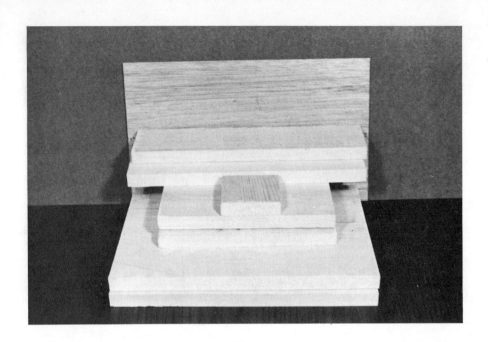

Procedure:

1. Cut all pieces to size and sand smooth.
2. Lay out the curvature for one of the sides on one of the 6½"×9" boards as shown in the picture.

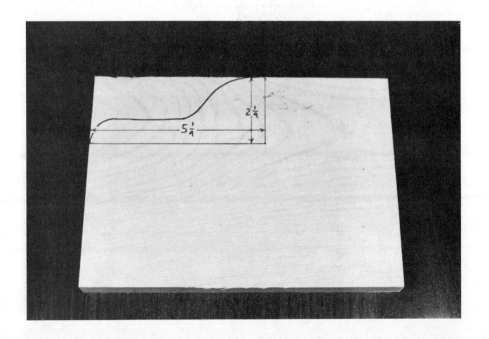

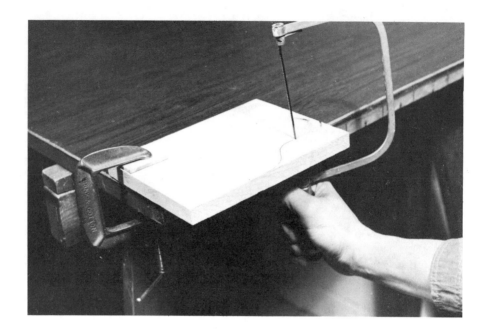

3. Clamp the board to the worktable and cut out the curve with a coping saw. Trace this design onto the other 6½"×9" board and cut to shape.

4. Lay out two holes on the 4"×5¼" board for a paper-clip holder by measuring in ¾ inch from each side and leaving ¾ inch between the two resulting 1½-inch by 2½-inch oblongs. Round off each corner of the holes with a ½-inch radius.

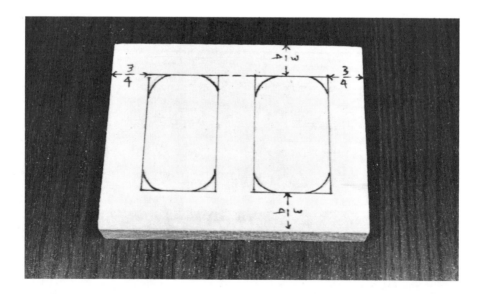

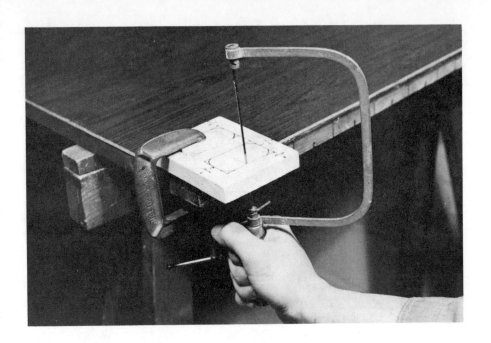

5. Clamp the piece to the worktable and drill a pilot hole into the center of each oblong. Insert the coping saw blade into the pilot holes and cut out the oblongs.

6. Lay out holes for a penholder on the $3'' \times 3''$ board by measuring in ⅝ inch from each side to find the center points for each corner hole. Then measure in ⅞ inch further to find the center points for the remaining holes.

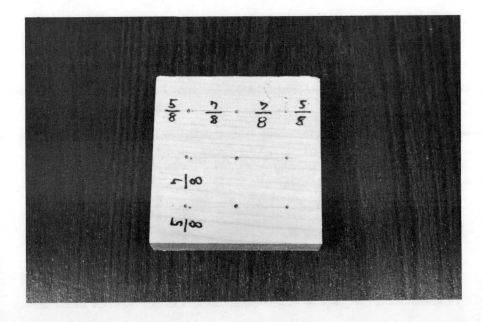

7. Clamp the wood to the worktable and drill ½-inch holes at each center point.
8. Drill shank holes into the side pieces, and pilot holes to match into the ends of the 9"×13" boards, which will be the bottom and shelf, so that the top of the shelf will be 3 inches below the top of the side pieces and the bottom is flush with the bottom of the sides.

9. Stain all pieces, and fasten the sides, bottom, and shelf together with 2″ handwrought nails.
10. Fasten the piece of plywood to the back of the sides, bottom, and shelf with ¾″ brads.

11. Attach the pen holder to one end of the 3″×13″ board, which will be a vertical partition, with 1¼″ brads.
12. Put the pen holder and partition into position between the sides and fasten with 1¼″ brads.

13. Place the paper-clip holder on the right end of the top shelf and fasten it with 1¼″ brads. Finish with a coat of clear lacquer. Allow at least four hours to dry and rub down with steel wool and wax.

TELEPHONE STAND

Materials:

Two 10"×30"×¾" pine boards
Three 10"×13½"×¾" pine boards
One 4"×13½"×¾" pine board
One 15"×26¼" plywood board
2" handwrought nails
¾" brads
Sandpaper
Stain and clear finish

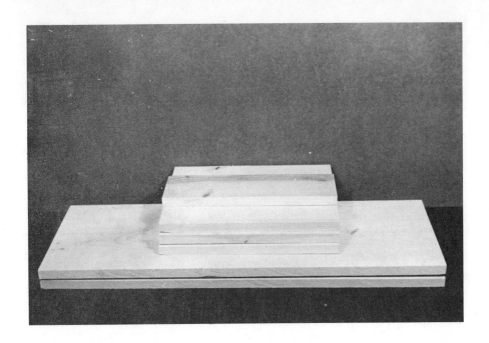

Description:

Every home can use a telephone stand. The shelf and book-rack incorporated in this design provide space for telephone books and your own special listings book.

Procedure:

1. Cut all pieces to overall size and sand smooth.
2. Lay out the curved shape for the top of the sides at one end of each of the 10″ by 30″ boards.

3. Clamp the wood to the worktable and cut out the curves with a coping saw.

4. Lay out a scallop shape on the bottom of the side pieces. Use a cardboard pattern to draw one half of the curve, then flip it over so both halves will be alike.

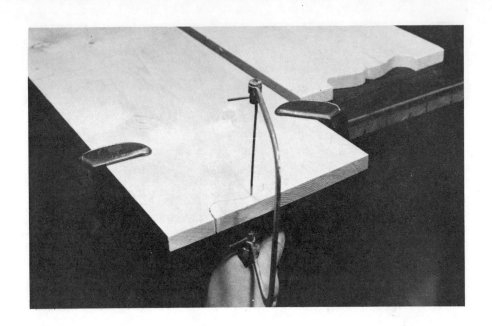

5. Clamp the wood to the worktable and cut out the scallop with the coping saw.

6. Lay out a scallop shape, similar to that on the side pieces but longer, centered along one side of the 4″×13½″ board, for the front bottom brace.

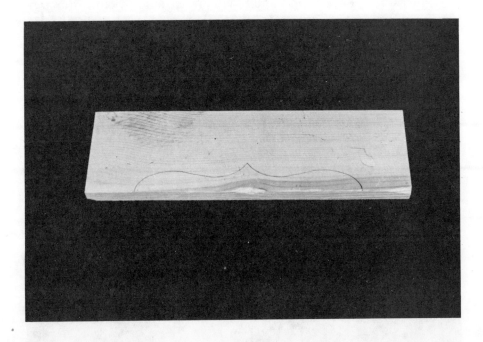

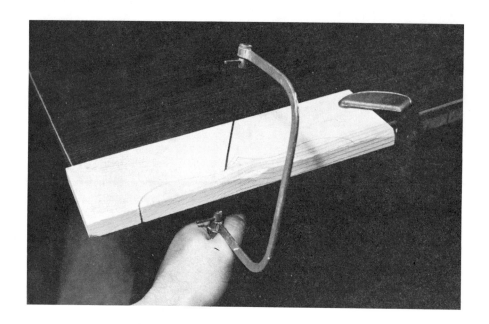

7. Clamp the wood to the worktable and cut out the scallop with the coping saw.

8. Drill shank holes into each side to fasten the three 10″×13½″ shelves and the bottom brace in place. The bottom shelf will be 4 inches from the bottom end of the sides. The top shelf will be 6 inches from the top end of the sides. The second shelf will be 4 inches below the top shelf. The brace will be flush with the bottom shelf and the bottom ends of the sides. Drill pilot holes into the shelves and the brace to match the shank holes.

9. Assemble sides, shelves, and brace, and fasten together with 2″ handwrought nails.
10. Attach the plywood board to the back of the stand with ¾″ brads. Stain and finish with clear lacquer, shellac, or varnish. Allow at least four hours to dry, and rub down with steel wool and wax. Polish with a rag.

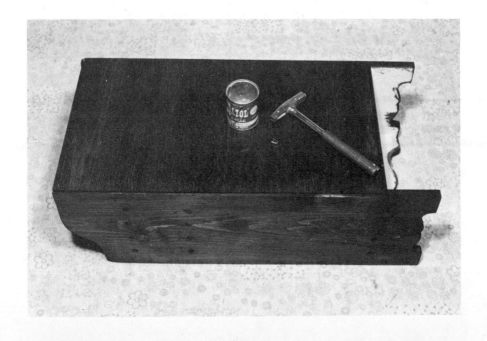

CHECKERBOARD AND CHECKERS

Materials:

Two 2"×12½"×¾" pine boards
Two 2"×14"×¾" pine boards
Two 14"×14"×¼" pieces of plywood or Masonite
Four 1"×14"×¾" pine boards
One 1½"×1½"×36" pine board
One 1"×1"×8" pine board
One pair of hinges (at least 3 inches in length)
Eight 2" handwrought nails
Contact cement
¾" brads
Sandpaper
Stain and clear finish

Description:

The uniqueness of this checkerboard is that it has its own storage compartment for holding checkers and chess pieces. The ½-inch-thick board squares were all cut from a 1½-inch-

square piece of pine. The ¼-inch thick checker pieces were all cut from a 1-inch-square piece of pine. To obtain squares and checkers of two different colors, half of the pieces were stained a dark walnut. Another method of obtaining the dark squares and checkers would be to use walnut or mahogany wood for the dark pieces, and a contrasting light-colored hardwood, such as cherry or maple, for the light pieces.

1. Cut the 2″×12½″ and 2″×14″ boards for the sides, and the plywood or Masonite for the top and bottom, to size. Sand the sides smooth.

2. Drill shank holes into the 14-inch sides ⅜ inch in from each end and 1 inch apart. Drill pilot holes into the ends of the 12½-inch sides to match the shank holes.

3. Assemble the four sides and fasten together with hand-wrought nails. Stain the sides.
4. Fasten one of the plywood or Masonite squares to the bottom of the box with 3/4" brads.

5. On 1½-inch-square stock, mark off every ½ inch until you have sixty-four pieces. Use a try square to extend these guide lines around three sides of the stock. Clamp the wood to the worktable and cut along each guide line with a handsaw.

6. Follow the same procedure to cut twenty-four checkers ¼-inch thick from 1-inch-square stock. Stain half of the checkers dark walnut.

7. Place a heavy coating of contact cement on one side of the remaining piece of plywood or Masonite, and the bottom and sides of each board square. Allow to dry for half an hour.

8. Cut the four 14-inch-long frame strips and miter the ends at a 45° angle. Line up the frame flush with the top and draw guide lines along the inside edges.

9. Place each square on the checkerboard and press firmly. Follow the guide line made on the top to assure that the squares form straight lines.

10. Allow at least two hours for the contact cement to dry. Sand the entire top surface of the squares with a rough-grade sandpaper until all saw-tooth marks are removed. Then use a medium-grade sandpaper, and finally a fine grade until the entire surface is smooth and the end grain shows clearly.

11. You can accentuate the lines between the rows of squares by cutting a shallow (1⁄16-inch) groove with a handsaw or a wood-carver's V-shaped veining tool. This will also help to prevent smudging the light squares as you stain the dark squares. Apply a dark stain to alternate squares.

12. Glue the frame into place around the checkerboard with contact cement. Align the top to the box and connect with a pair of hinges. A coating of clear lacquer, varnish, or shellac can be applied to all wood surfaces. Allow four hours for drying, and then rub down with steel wool and wax. Polish with a rag.

TOOL CADDY

Materials:

Two 4"×30"×2" pine boards
Two 4"×24"×¾" pine boards
Two 4"×11"×¾" pine boards
One 9½"×24"×¾" pine board
One 1½"×24"×¾" pine board
One 7½"×30"×¼" piece of plywood or Masonite
Two ½"×30"×¾" pine boards

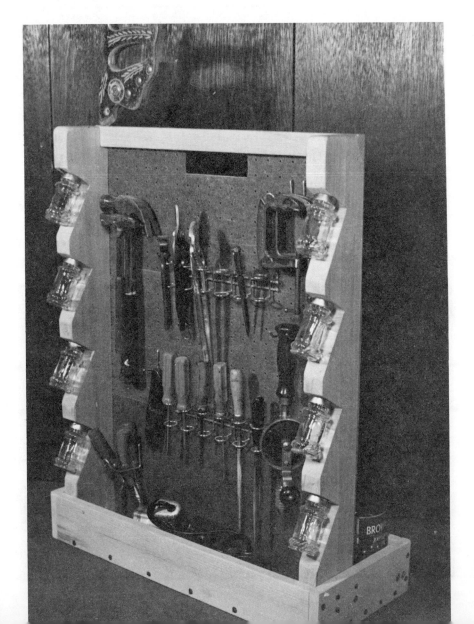

One 24″×30″×⅛″ pegboard
Eight baby-food jars
2″ handwrought nails
2″ brads
1″ flat-head nails
Hooks of various shapes for hanging tools
Sandpaper
Clear finish

Description:

It is a great frustration for any craftsperson not to have tools readily available at the moment they are needed. One way of avoiding this frustration is to build yourself a tool caddy which will hold the most commonly used tools. This tool caddy is large enough to hold a fairly large assortment of tools but small enough to carry around. The pegboard will allow tools to be hung in an organized manner. The base will hold cans for nails and other large hardware. The jars can hold small screws, nuts, washers, and similar hardware.

Procedure:

1. Cut all pieces to overall size and sand smooth.

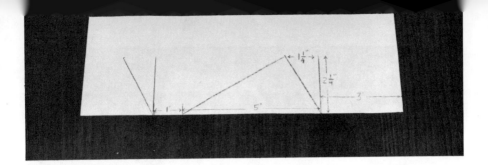

2. Lay out and cut the pattern for the zigzag cutouts on the upright sides from a piece of cardboard.

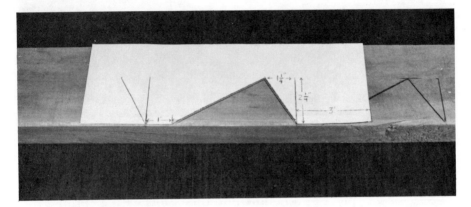

3. Trace the pattern for the upright sides on the 4"×30" boards, starting at the top. Place the cutout part of the pattern at the base of the previously drawn section and repeat the pattern until you have four cutouts.

4. Clamp the wood to the worktable and cut out each zigzag with a handsaw.

5. At the top, back corner of each upright side piece cut out a slot for the handle ¾ inch by 1½ inches. Nail the 1½"×24" piece as a handle into these slots with 2" brads.

6. Fasten the pegboard to the sides with 1" flat-head nails. Using a coping saw, cut out a hole 1 inch by 6 inches in the pegboard, centered and next to the handle.

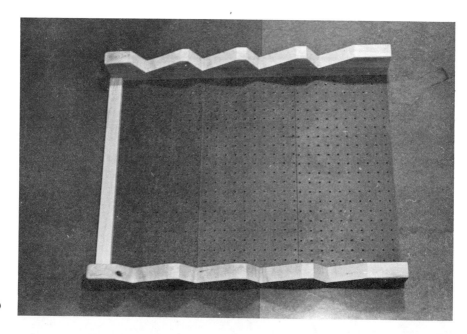

7. Assemble a saw crib by fastening the ½″×30″ strips down the sides of the plywood or Masonite with 1″ flat-head nails. Line up one side of the saw crib with the back edge of one of the upright sides and fasten with 2″ brads. Fasten the other side of the saw crib to the pegboard with 1″ flat-head nails, nailing through the pegboard into the side piece of the saw crib.

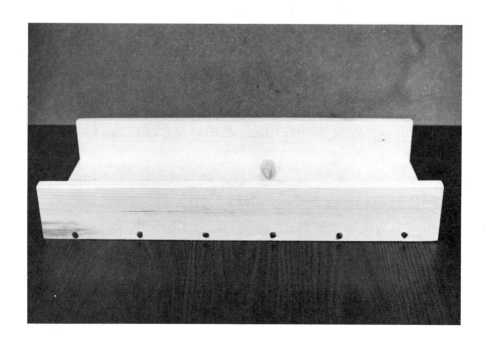

8. Drill shank holes along one side of each of the 4″×24″ boards, and pilot holes into the edges of the 9½″×24″ board to match, and fasten them together with 2″ handwrought nails to make the sides and bottom of the base.

9. Attach the 4″×11″ boards in the same way to make the ends of the base.

10. Drill shank holes into the ends of the base and pilot holes to match into the bottom of the upright sides, and fasten them together with 2″ handwrought nails.

11. Fasten jar tops with screws to the top of the cutouts in the upright sides. Screw the jars into the tops. Hang hooks on the pegboard.

12. Apply a few coats of clear finish to wood surfaces.

PIPE RACK

Materials:

Two 6″×12¼″×¾″ pine boards
One 1¾″×18½″×¾″ pine board
One 4¼″×18½″×¾″ pine board
One 6″×18½″×¾″ pine board
1½″ round-head screws
Sandpaper
Stain and clear finish

Description:

This simple pipe rack is long and narrow and was designed to be hung on a wall or set on a mantel over a fireplace. It will hold twenty pipes but you can adjust the design to hold more or fewer pipes as desired.

Procedure:

1. Cut all pieces to overall size and sand smooth.
2. To lay out the curvature of the sides, draw a 1-inch grid on a piece of cardboard and draw the design.

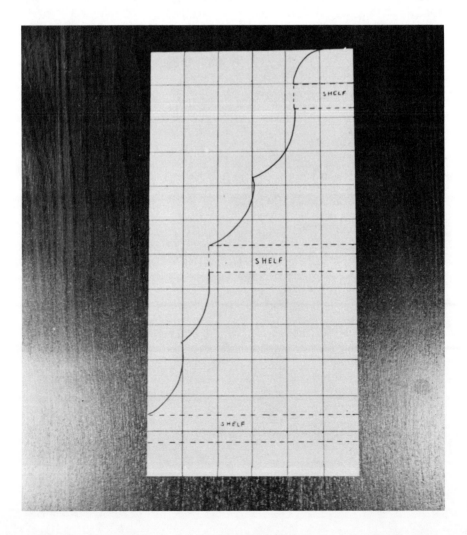

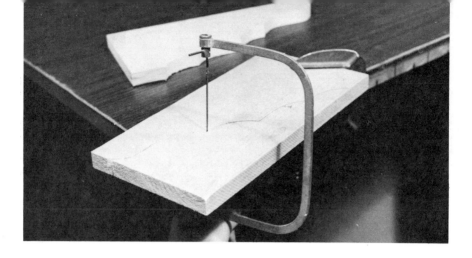

3. Cut out the shape of the cardboard and transfer the design to the 6"×12¼" boards.

4. Clamp the wood to the worktable and cut out the curves with a coping saw.

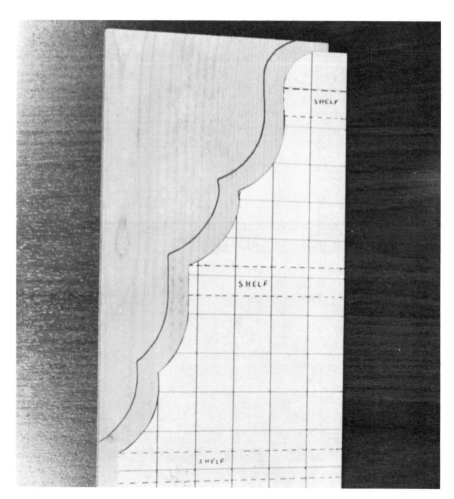

5. Lay out the three shelves in preparation for drilling and cutting out the holes by following the diagram.

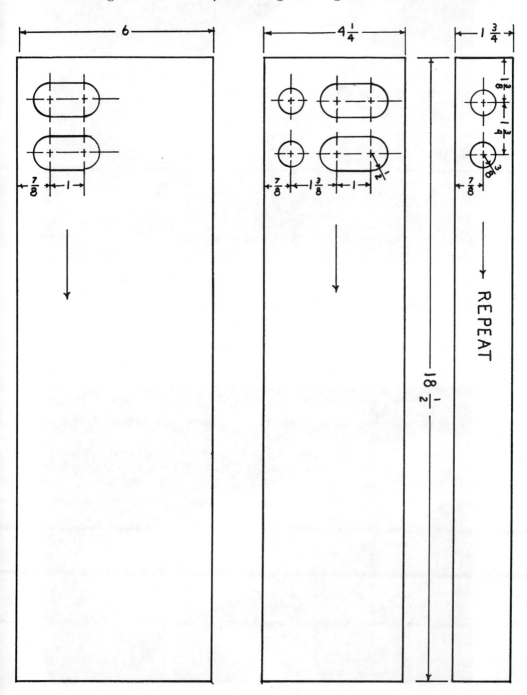

6. Clamp the wood to the worktable and bore out the stem holes with a ¾″ bit.
7. Cut out the bowl holes with the coping saw.

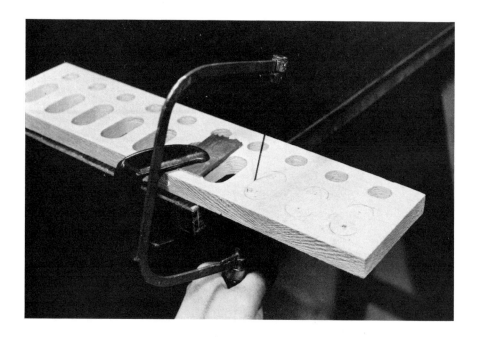

8. Drill shank holes in the side pieces, and pilot holes into the ends of the shelves to match. The bottom shelf is placed 1 inch from the bottom of the sides. The middle shelf is placed 4 inches above the bottom shelf. The top shelf is placed 4 inches above the middle shelf. Assemble and fasten together with 1½″ round-head screws.

9. Stain and finish with a clear lacquer, varnish, or shellac.

BIRDHOUSE

Materials:

Two 12″×19″×¾″ pine boards
One 6″×19″×¾″ pine board
One 6″×4¾″×¾″ pine board
One 6″×8″×¾″ pine board
One 6″×5″×¾″ pine board
One 6″×4″×¾″ pine board
One 6″×8¾″×¾″ pine board
One 6″×1″×¾″ pine board
Nineteen 1½″×8″×⅛″ pine boards
Four dowels 2½″×¼″
2″ brads
¾″ brads
Sandpaper
Glue
Exterior stain or paint

Description:

This cottage-style birdhouse includes a feeder on one end and can hold four small birds' nests for sparrows or wrens. It can be mounted on top of a post or can be attached to the side of a house, barn, garage, tool shed, or tree. Ideally it should be constructed of redwood or cedar because these woods withstand weather very well. You can also use pine, but an exterior-type stain or other finish should be applied as a preservative.

Procedure:

1. Cut all pieces to overall size.

2. Lay out the shape of the front and the placement of the entrance holes on one of the 12″×19″ boards as indicated in the diagram.

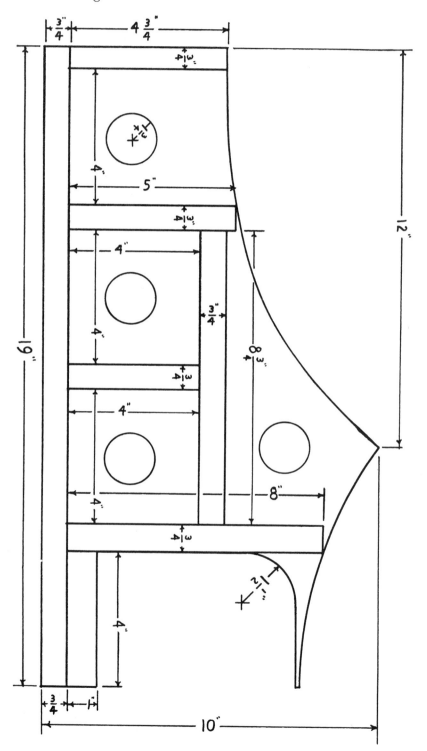

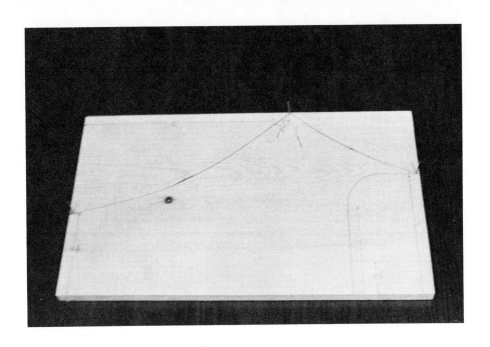

3. Hammer in nails at the three points of the roof. These will be used as an aid to make the curves of the roof.
4. Bend a thin strip of wood or wooden carpenter's yardstick between the nails at the left and top edges and draw a curved line. The curve should intersect the point of placement for the 5-inch partition.

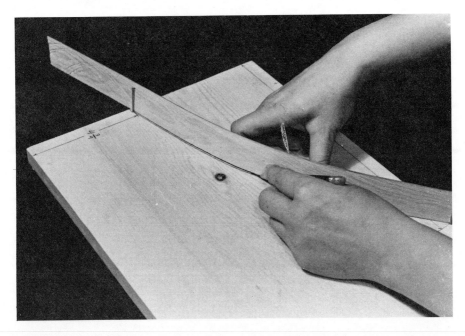

5. Repeat step 4 to make the curve between the nails at the top and right edges.

6. Clamp the wood to the worktable and cut out the curves of the roof and the shape of the feeder with a coping saw. Trace the shape of the front onto the other $12'' \times 19''$ board for the back piece. Cut out the shape of the back with the coping saw.

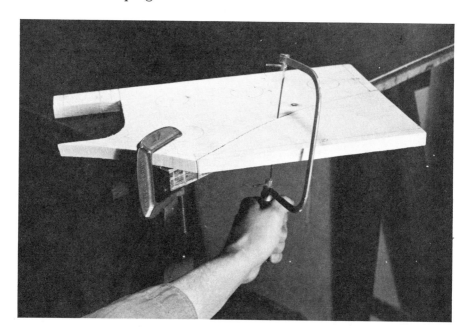

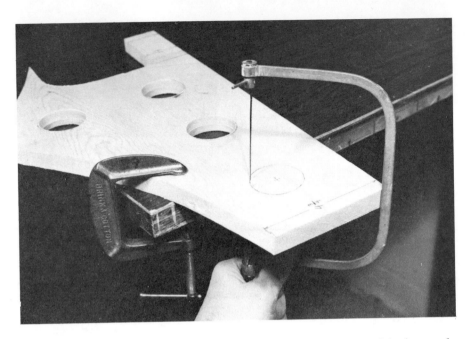

7. Drill pilot holes for insertion of the coping saw blade, and cut out the entrance holes.
8. Drill ¼-inch holes for the dowels ½ inch below the entrance holes.

9. Assemble the 6″×4¾″ left end piece, the 6″×4″ middle partition, and the 6″×19″ base. The right side of the middle partition should be placed 8¾ inches from the right end of the base. Fasten together with 2″ brads.

10. Assemble the 6″×5″ left partition, the 6″×8″ right partition, and the 6″×8¾″ second-floor piece. The floor should be placed 4 inches from the bottom of each partition. Fasten together with 2″ brads.

11. Assemble the second-floor section and the base section so that the 8-inch partition is 4 inches from the left end of the base. Fasten together with 2″ brads.

12. Attach the back piece to the base and partitions with 2″ brads.

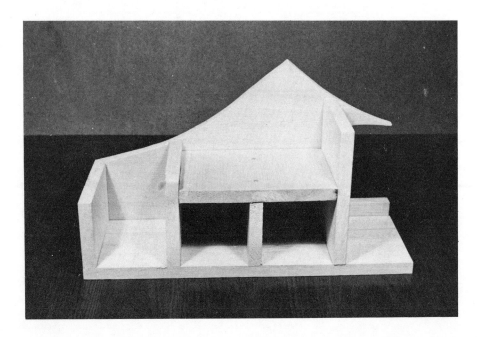

13. Fasten on the front piece with 2″ brads.
14. Put the 6″×1″ piece in place at the end of the feeder and fasten it with 2″ brads.

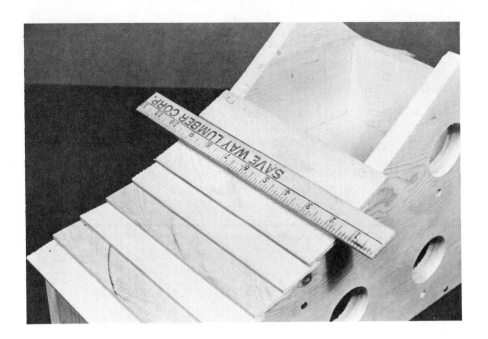

15. Place the first roof board so that it overhangs the left end by ½ inch and the front and back equally, and fasten it with ¾″ brads. Each succeeding roof board should overlap the preceding board by ¼ inch. A guide strip can be used to line up each roof board so that they will all be parallel to each other. Overlapping the boards will keep the rain out of the interior compartments.
16. Fasten the dowels in place with glue. Finish with an exterior stain or finish.

INDEX

Adjustable book rack, 56–62
Alcohol, to clean brushes, 26

Baseball game, 29–36
Benzine, to clean brushes, 26
Birdhouse, 120–29
Boards, 23–24
    bread slicing, 37–40
    chopping, 41–44
Book rack, adjustable, 56–62
Boxes
    ecology, 67–72
    shoeshine, 79–85
Brace and bit, 13
Bracket and shelf, 50–55
Brads, 19
Brass screws, 21
Bread slicing board, 37–40
Bronze screws, 21
Brushes, cleaning, 26

Calendar, perpetual, 45–49
C-clamp, 14–15
Cedar, for birdhouse, 121
Ceramic tiles, planter with, 63–66
Checkerboard and checkers, 100–6
Cherry wood
    for bread slicing board, 37
    for chopping board, 41
Chisels, 8
Chopping board, 41–44
Clamp, C-, 14–15
Coffee cup rack, 73–78
Combination square, 15
Common nail, 19

Compass, 17–18
Contact cement, 20
Countersink, 11
Crosscut saws, 5, 6
Cup rack, coffee, 73–78
Curves, drawing, 18

Desk organizer, 86–93
Dividers, 18
Dowels, 22
Drills, 10–13
    drilling a hole, 12–13
    inserting a bit, 11

Ecology box, 67–72
Edge grain, 23
Elmer's glue, 20
End grain, 23

Fastenings, 19–22
    dowels, 22
    glue, 20
    nails, 2–4, 19
    screws, 21–22
Finishing nails, 19
Fir, 23

Games
    baseball, 29–36
    checkerboard and checkers,
        100–6
Glue, 20
Gouges, 8
Grain, 23

Hammers, 1–4
  assembling two pieces of wood,
    3–4
  pulling out nails, 2–3
  starting nails, 2
Hand drill, 11
Hardwoods, 23
  cherry, 37, 41
  walnut, 37, 41, 63
Hemlock, 23

Kitchen, working in, ix–x
Knots, 24

Lacquer, 25, 27
  and cleaning brushes, 26
Lumber, 23–24

Maple, 23
Measuring and marking, tips on,
    18
Miter box, 17

Nails, 19
  and assembling two pieces of
    wood, 3–4
  pulling out, 2–3
  starting, 2
Nail set, 19

Oak, 23

Painting, 25–26, 27
Pegboard, for tool caddy, 108
Perpetual calendar, 45–49
Phillips screwdriver, 4
Pine, 23
Pipe rack, 114–19
Planes, 9–10
  how to square off a block of
    wood, 9–10
Planter with tiles, 63–66

Racks
  book rack, 56–62
  desk organizer, 86–93
  coffee cup rack, 73–78
  pipe rack, 114–19
  telephone stand, 94–99

tool caddy, 107–13
Redwood, for birdhouse, 121
Rip saws, 5, 6

Sanding, 26, 27
Saws, 5–7
  coping, 7
  how to use, 6
Screwdrivers, 4
Screw hanger, 51
Screws, 21–22
Shellac, 25, 27
  and cleaning brushes, 26
Shelves
  bracket and shelf, 50–55
  desk organizer, 86–93
  telephone stand, 94–99
Shoeshine box, 79–85
Smoothing plane, 9–10
Softwoods, 23
  cedar, 121
  redwood, 121
Spruce, 23
Squares, try, 15–16
  how to square a board, 16
Staining, 25, 27
Steel screws, 21

Table, for working, ix–x
Tape measure, steel, 16
Telephone stand, 94–99
Tiles, planter with, 63–66
Tool caddy, 107–13
Try squares, 15–16
  how to square a board, 16
Turpentine, to clean brushes, 26

Varnishing, 25, 27

Walnut, 23
  for bread slicing board, 37
  for chopping board, 41
  for planter with tiles, 63
Waterproof glue, 20
Wood, 23–24
Wood finishing, 25–27
  basic procedures, 26–27
  helpful hints, 26
Wood screws, 21

FRANK D. TORRE is an avid do-it-yourselfer. He has made many things for his home, including an extension for his house that is larger than the house itself. His carving endeavors include his dining-room table, some lamps, and a crib for his young son.

Mr. Torre is the principal of BOCES Wilson Tech in Lindenhurst, New York, and has received the Ed. D. degree from New York University. He lives in Northport, New York, with his wife and two sons.